Robin Page

SHALL WE DANCE?

Beach Lane Books
New York London Toronto Sydney New Delhi

The side-to-side shuffle of a bird of paradise, the wiggle of a peacock spider's tail, or the wave of a fiddler crab's claw—in the animal world, these displays are just the thing to attract a partner. To have babies and start a family, animals need to find a mate, and many creatures begin their courtship by performing a dance. Males are often more colorful and flamboyant than their female partners, who need to avoid attention in order to survive and raise their young. So when it comes to courtship rituals, it's usually the male that makes the first move. Dancing—which can include an intricate series of steps, gestures, and sounds—shows off a male's strength, fitness, and ability to make a good father. If a female likes his moves, she may join him in a duet.

Courtship is the reason most animals dance. But some creatures dance to signal to others in their group or simply as a way of moving from place to place. Whatever the reason for a spin, strut, or shimmy, the complex steps of an animal's dance are fascinating. . . .

Boobies high-step.

A male **blue-footed booby** starts things off by presenting his love interest with a gift, usually a stick or a stone. Next, he strikes a handsome pose with his beak pointing skyward while he makes a whistling sound. The finale is a high-stepping dance that shows off his bright blue feet. If he performs well—and if his feet are blue enough—an impressed female booby will join him in the dance.

Finches tap.

Blue-capped finches begin their courtship by exchanging a piece of nesting material with their future mate. What follows is singing, bobbing, and even a bit of tap dancing. By keeping this passionate dance up for a long time, the two birds prove to each other that they are strong and fit and will make good parents.

Mandarinfish flaunt.

At twilight, **mandarinfish** begin their courtship. Females swim to a coral reef where males gather and show off their fins and flaunt their bright colors. If a male is large, colorful, and aggressive enough, a female will let him chase her. If things go according to plan, she will join him for a swim.

Seahorses twine.

A male **Barbour's seahorse** spends days wooing a female, often joining her in a ritual dance. Entwining their tails, the little fish synchronize their moves. Following a number of these dances, the male seahorse receives the female's eggs in a special pouch on his belly. He will keep the eggs safe until they hatch.

And ostriches
thump!

When a male **ostrich** is intrigued by a female, he begins kneeling. Then he fluffs his feathers, flaps his wings, and moves his head from side to side. To finish his dance, he makes a loud thumping sound by hitting his head against his back.

Cottontails tumble.

Male and female **cottontails** perform an athletic courtship dance. There is running, racing, and even boxing. If both rabbits seem interested, the next step is to take turns jumping and tumbling over each other. That's a sure way to bond if you're a cottontail.

Sifakas prance.

Standing upright, a male and female **crowned sifaka** prance gracefully on the forest floor. With their short arms and long legs, their ability to move on all fours is limited to the trees. Their balletic moves are not performed to attract a mate. They are simply a way to get around in their forest habitat.

Turtles tickle.

For a **red-eared slider**, tickling is the best way to win a mate. The male turtle—and sometimes the female—tries to charm a mate by approaching them underwater. The turtles flutter their claws on each other's faces, tickling gently. This courtship ritual may be just the right touch for charming a future partner.

Eagles cartwheel.

Bald eagles court a mate with a playful chase high above the earth. They lock talons and begin cartwheeling, spinning in the air as they plummet toward the ground. Just in time, the birds break apart and soar higher into the sky.

And
flamingos
march!

If an **Andean flamingo** wants to attract a mate, he or she will need an array of dance moves. There's flagging—turning their head from side to side—marching, rushing back and forth, and finally, wing saluting. With luck, one special flamingo will approve.

Frogs flag.

Foot-flagging is how the male **Indian dancing frog** gets a female's attention. These frogs live near noisy, fast-flowing streams, where the croaking call of a male frog can't be heard. He hopes a female will see him!

Mudskippers leap.

Male **blue-spotted mudskippers** develop vibrant spots on their bodies to entice females. Flaring his fins and leaping high into the air, a mudskipper performs an acrobatic dance. He lands with a loud splash in an attempt to attract a mate. If she's impressed, she will accompany him to his burrow.

Sage grouses strut.

Every spring in the American West, male **greater sage grouses** gather on their traditional dancing grounds to strut for females. A male's dance consists of puffing up his chest, inflating his large yellow neck pouches, spreading his spiky tail feathers, and making a lot of noise.

Springboks pronk.

By pronking—jumping straight up in the air—the **springbok** may be showing off for a future mate. This performance shows how fit this antelope is and proves that he or she would be an excellent choice to help raise a family.

And humpback whales waltz!

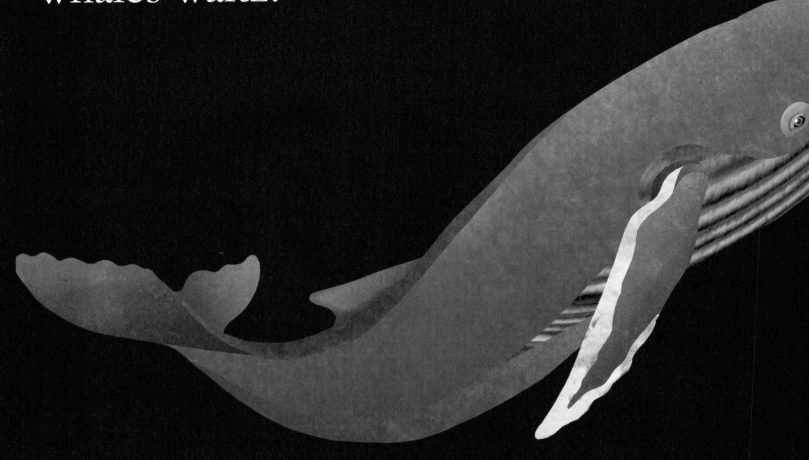

A male **humpback whale** initiates a romance with a song that can travel for many miles. If this melody attracts a female, the two will perform a slow-motion dance together—twisting, twirling, circling, and diving around each other. They are incredibly graceful as they waltz deep in the ocean.

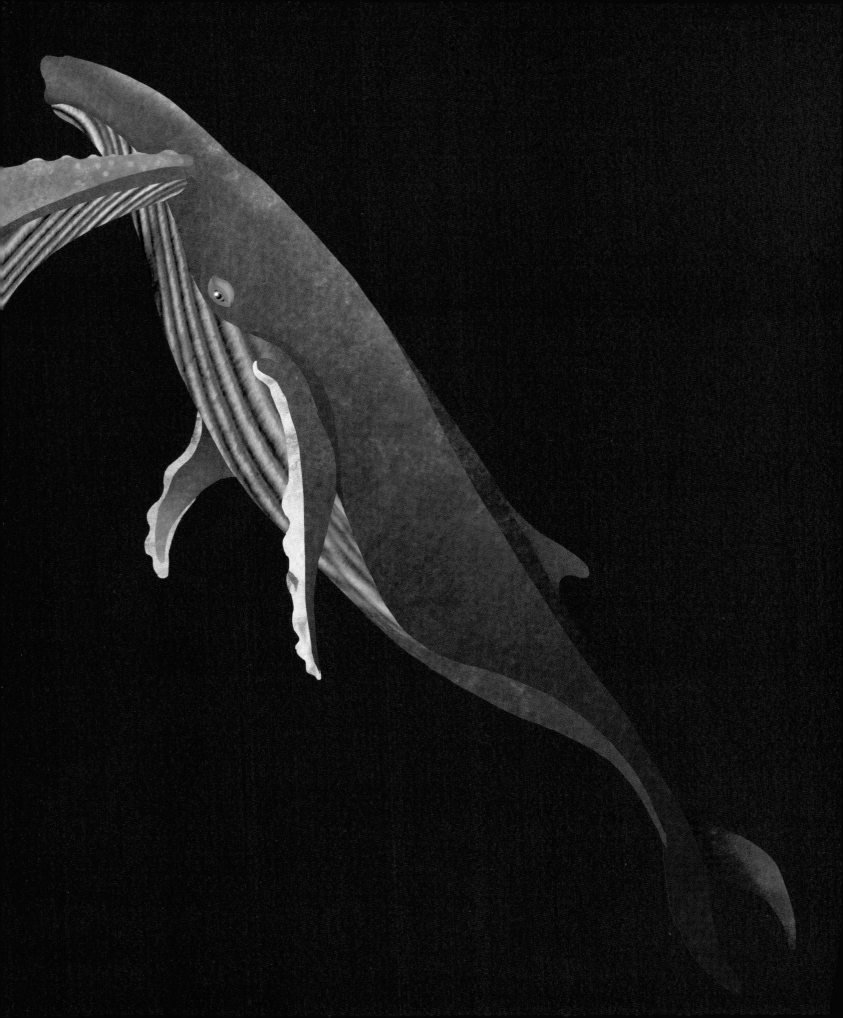

Crabs wave.

Waving its large claw, a male **fiddler crab** signals a prospective mate. This display—combined with a drumming noise the crab makes by rubbing his claws together—takes a lot of strength. It shows the female that he is physically fit and will be a good father. If he meets her expectations, she joins him in his burrow. His show was a success!

Newts shimmy.

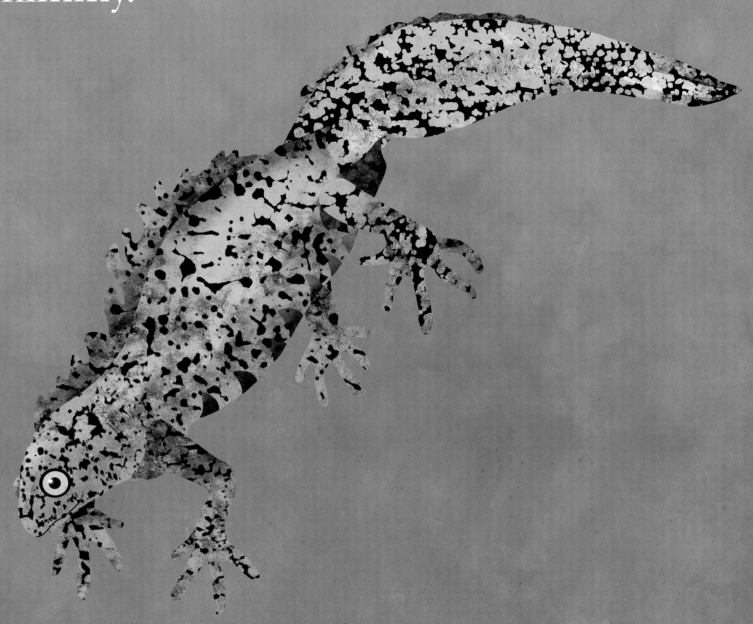

As the first step in luring a female, the **great crested newt** grows a large crest along his back. This takes a lot of energy, and a big crest shows that he is healthy and strong. But he also must perform. If a female appears interested, he shimmies his tail, creating waves that sometimes push her backward through the water.

Walruses clap.

To display his fitness to a potential mate or rival, a male **walrus** produces a rhythmic sound by clapping his front flippers. The sound is very loud, and he may continue this serenade day and night for as long as a month.

Hummingbirds dazzle.

The male **calliope hummingbird** tries to dazzle a female. He flashes his magenta throat feathers and flies back and forth, looping and zigzagging. If the female is inspired by his strength and skill, she will join him in flight.

And
scorpions
tango!

As a male **Asian forest scorpion** approaches a female, he waves his pincers, swings his tail back and forth, and shivers his body. If she responds to his gestures, he hooks his pincers to hers and holds on tightly. Then the tango begins.

Lesser floricans spring.

During the rainy monsoon season, a pair of **lesser floricans** joins in a courtship ritual. The female—hardly visible in the tall grass—makes a whistling sound, her way of calling a mate. The male then performs an amazing aerial display. Leaping straight up, he arches his neck backward to display his impressive plumage. He may leap five hundred times in a day, reaching heights of more than six feet.

Sticklebacks zigzag.

The male **three-spined stickleback** attracts a female with his bright orange throat and belly and a well-built nest. He performs a zigzag dance, trying to charm his prospective mate. If she's impressed, she'll enter the tunnel he's made in his nest. Next, he'll vibrate the female's tail to stimulate egg laying. He fertilizes the eggs immediately. The male may perform this task several more times, growing his nest of eggs. Male sticklebacks care for and protect the eggs and offspring.

Birds of paradise waggle.

Carola's Parotia, a bird of paradise, is sometimes called the king of dancers. With a series of moves performed in a precise sequence, he bounces, flutters, sways, and poses, all leading up to his finale—spreading his feathers to look like a tutu. He will waggle for the females perched on a branch above him, hoping one will be amazed by his dance.

Spiders wiggle.

As a male **peacock spider** dances for his love interest, he lifts his tail-flap and wiggles his third set of legs to and fro. But he doesn't stop there—he also sings, scrapes, clicks, and taps. This produces vibrations that are sensed by the female. It's important that she's impressed. Otherwise, she might decide to devour him.

And praying mantises flash!

A male **praying mantis** raises his wings, flashes his eyespots, and swings his abdomen back and forth. He's trying to entice a potential mate. If she is interested, she will return his gesture. If he's lucky, she'll be well fed and won't eat him.

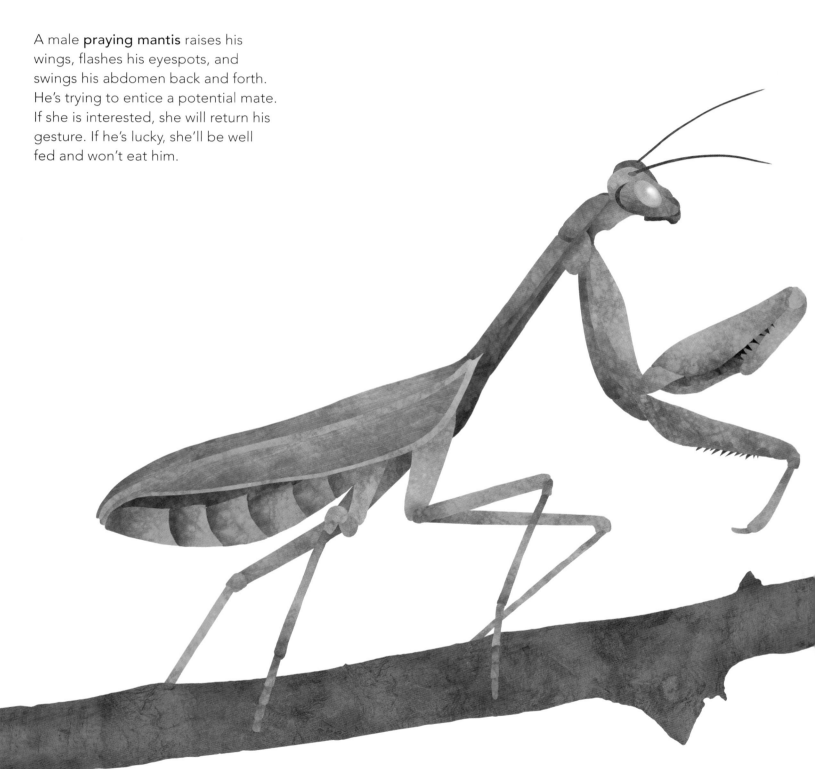

Dolphins spin.

Spinner dolphins leap out of the water in unison. They synchronize their movements, jumping over and over and spinning as many as seven times before reentering the water. These leaps may signal dominance or warn of danger—or maybe they're just playing.

Devil rays launch.

Devil rays gather in huge numbers and launch themselves out of the water. They jump high above the surface, flipping and somersaulting before splashing down. This action might help get rid of parasites, but it also may be a form of courtship.

Grebes glide.

Rising high in the water, a pair of **Western grebes** performs what is called a rush, gliding across the surface of a lake as if it were a ballroom floor. This mating dance ends with a coordinated dive into the water.

Cranes pirouette.

Male and female **red-crowned cranes** begin their partnership by calling to each other. The cranes—sometimes known as snow ballerinas—bow, bob, pose, and pirouette. They perform these amazing ballet moves many times, repeating them over the years to create a lifelong bond.

And baby cranes
pirouette too!

Baby **red-crowned cranes** start practicing their dance moves just a few days after they are born. They bow, bob, pose, and pirouette just like adult cranes. The cranes will continue to rehearse their dance until they become adults. Practice makes perfect!

BEACH LANE BOOKS

An imprint of Simon & Schuster Children's Publishing Division. • 1230 Avenue of the Americas, New York, New York 10020 • © 2023 by Robin Page • Book design by Robin Page © 2023 by Simon & Schuster, Inc. • All rights reserved, including the right of reproduction in whole or in part in any form. • BEACH LANE BOOKS and colophon are trademarks of Simon & Schuster, Inc. • For information about special discounts for bulk purchases, please contact Simon & Schuster Special Sales at 1-866-506-1949 or business@simonandschuster.com. • The Simon & Schuster Speakers Bureau can bring authors to your live event. For more information or to book an event, contact the Simon & Schuster Speakers Bureau at 1-866-248-3049 or visit our website at www.simonspeakers.com. • The text for this book was set in Avenir, Garamond and Helvetica Neue. • The illustrations for this book were rendered in Adobe Photoshop. • Manufactured in China • 1122 SCP • First Edition • 10 9 8 7 6 5 4 3 2 1 • Library of Congress Cataloging-in-Publication Data • Names: Page, Robin, 1957- author. • Title: Shall we dance? / Robin Page. • Description: New York : Beach Lane Books, 2023. | Includes bibliographical references. | Audience: Ages 4-8 | Audience: Grades 2-3 | Summary: "Nature is putting on a dance recital...come watch! From award-winning author-illustrator Robin Page, SHALL WE DANCE? is a beautiful exploration of how and why different animals move their bodies. Whether it's to find a mate, repel a predator, or just for fun, readers will learn the reason and purpose behind each animal and critter's graceful, exuberant, or playful moves. And they might even want to get up and join in the dancing fun!"— Provided by publisher. • Identifiers: LCCN 2022008058 (print) | LCCN 2022008059 (ebook) | ISBN 9781665916059 (hardcover) | ISBN 9781665916066 (ebook) • Subjects: LCSH: Courtship in animals—Juvenile literature. | Animal behavior—Juvenile literature. • Classification: LCC QL761 .P35 2023 (print) | LCC QL761 (ebook) | DDC 591.5—dc23/eng/20220528 • LC record available at https://lccn.loc.gov/2022008058 • LC ebook record available at https://lccn.loc.gov/2022008059

SELECTED SOURCES

Braaf, Ellen R. *Dances with Animals*. Northampton, MA: Pioneer Valley Educational Press, Inc., 2015.

Kaner, Etta, and Marilyn Faucher. *Animals Do, Too!: How They Behave Just like You*. Toronto, ON: Kids Can Press, 2017.

Knight, Tim. *Dramatic Displays*. Oxford: Heinemann Library, 2004.

Knight, Tim. *Amazing Nature*. Chicago, IL: Heinemann Library, 2003.

Prasadam-Halls, Smriti, and Florence Weiser. *Dancing Birds and Singing Apes: How Animals Say I Love You*. London, UK: Hodder Wayland, 2022.

von der Gathen, Katharina, Anke Kuhl, and Shelley Tanaka. *Do Animals Fall in Love?* Wellington, New Zealand: Gecko Press, 2021.

West, Krista. *Animal Behavior: Animal Courtship*. New York, NY: Chelsea House Pub, 2009.

In Memory of Steve